The Mortgage Mastery System

KYLA LOVELL

Copyright © 2024 Kyla Lovell

All rights reserved.

ISBN: 978-1-7382251-2-5

Contents

1 INTRODUCTION TO MORTGAGES 1
    Definition of Mortgages 1
    The Role of Mortgages in The Canadian Real Estate Industry 1
    An Overview of Canada's Mortgage History 2

2 THE MORTGAGE LANDSCAPE IN CANADA 3
    An Overview of The Housing Market in Canada 3
    Impact of Recession on Mortgages 3

3 TYPES OF MORTGAGES 5
    Fixed-Rate Mortgages 5
    Variable-Rate Mortgages 7
    Hybrid Mortgages 9
    Open and Closed Mortgages 10

4 CHOOSING THE RIGHT MORTGAGE 14
    Factors to Consider When Choosing a Mortgage Product 14
    Assessing Individual Financial Goals and Risk Tolerance 15
    Understanding Mortgage Terms and Conditions 15
    Affordability and The Mortgage Pre-Approval Process 16
    How To Compare Mortgage Products And Lenders 17

5 MORTGAGE PROTECTION AND RISK MITIGATION 18
    The Significance of Mortgage Insurance 18
    Role of CMHC (Canada Mortgage and Housing Corporation) 19
    Strategies For Reducing Mortgage Risks 19
    Exploring the Benefits of Fixed-Rate Mortgages 20
    Lessons from the 2008 Global Financial Crisis 20

6 UNDERSTANDING RECESSIONS AND MORTGAGES 22

    Overview of the 2008 Global Financial Crisis 22

    Impacts on the Canadian Housing Market and Mortgages 23

    Lessons Learned and Implications for Future Mortgage Decisions 24

    The Role of Government Interventions and Regulations 24

    Case Study of the 1991 Downturn: The Canadian Experience with Recessions and Mortgages 25

    Government Responses and Effects on the Mortgage Market 25

    Key Takeaways for Mortgage Borrowers During Economic Downturns 26

7 NAVIGATING THE MORTGAGE PROCESS 28

    Step-by-Step Guide to Obtaining a Mortgage 28

    Documentation and Requirements 29

    Mortgage Application Tips 30

    Common Pitfalls to Avoid During the Mortgage Process 31

    Closing the Mortgage and Post-Mortgage Considerations 32

8 BUILDING WEALTH THROUGH MORTGAGES 33

    Overview of How Mortgages Can Be Used to Build Wealth in Canada . 33

    Strategies for Leveraging Mortgages to Invest in Real Estate in Canada 33

9 THE FUTURE OF MORTGAGES IN CANADA 36

    Predictions for the Future of Mortgages 37

    Regulatory Changes and Their Potential Impact on Borrowers 37

CONCLUSION 39

APPENDIX 40

    Glossary of Mortgage-Related Terms 40

    Additional Resources and References 41

NOTES 42

1 INTRODUCTION TO MORTGAGES

Definition of Mortgages

A mortgage is a loan arrangement that allows a borrower to buy real estate. It is a financial arrangement between the lender and the borrower. This kind of loan uses the asset purchased as collateral, giving the lender security if the borrower defaults. The borrower receives funding from the lender, typically a banking institution or credit union, enabling them to finish the transaction. After that, the borrower makes consistent payments over a defined length of time, covering both interest and principal, until the mortgage is paid in full.

Typically, mortgages are long-term obligations that last between 15 and 30 years. The mortgage agreement contains information on the conditions of the loan, such as the repayment schedule and any special requirements. As a borrower, you should carefully read over and fully understand these conditions before signing a mortgage contract.

The Role of Mortgages in The Canadian Real Estate Industry

The Canadian real estate industry, a significant driver of the nation's economy, depends heavily on mortgages. Mortgages provide the tools to accomplish homeownership, a significant financial aim for most Canadians. By providing financing options, mortgages enable families and individuals to buy homes and gradually accumulate wealth.

In Canada, there is a significant demand for mortgages since many residents need to borrow money to cover the high cost of homeownership. Mortgages make homeownership more affordable by providing the required finances upfront and allowing buyers to stretch out the payments over a more extended period. Furthermore, the availability of mortgage financing increases demand for homes, which boosts the expansion of the building and real estate sectors and other industries.

Furthermore, the stability and robustness of the mortgage industry in Canada support economic stability at all levels. Governmental organizations like the Canada Mortgage and Housing Corporation (CMHC) and the Office of the Superintendent of Financial Institutions (OSFI) oversee mortgage lending to maintain responsible lending practices and sound financial stability in the mortgage sector. This reduces risks and ensures a stable housing market.

An Overview of Canada's Mortgage History

Mortgages have been a part of Canadian history since the earliest days of European colonization. Colonial administrations primarily utilized mortgages to finance infrastructure development and encourage colonization then. As the population increased, mortgages became more widely available to individual borrowers, which promoted homeownership and the growth of towns.

Mortgage financing further advanced in Canada in the 19th century with the establishment of chartered banks. By expanding to provide mortgage loans to private customers, these banks increased the number of people who could become homeowners. Mortgages were essential to the expansion of residential real estate and the growth of the economy in metropolitan areas.

The Canadian mortgage market kept changing during the 20th century. Government measures and regulations were put in place to protect borrowers and keep the housing market stable. For instance, mortgage insurance was introduced in 1946 with the establishment of the Canada Mortgage and Housing Corporation (CMHC), giving lenders greater confidence and safeguarding against default risks.

The Canadian mortgage industry has seen tremendous expansion and innovation in recent years. Banking institutions provide a range of mortgage options to meet the different demands of borrowers, such as fixed, viable-rate and hybrid mortgages. To further improve accessibility to homeownership, government initiatives have been implemented to encourage first-time buyers, such as the First-Time Home Buyer Incentive.

Knowledge of the Canadian mortgage industry's history might help you better understand the forces influencing the mortgage market today. It can help borrowers recognize the advancements made in mortgage financing, the policies implemented, and the general reliability of the Canadian real estate market.

2 THE MORTGAGE LANDSCAPE IN CANADA

An Overview of The Housing Market in Canada

Housing in Canada is a vibrant and diverse sector that includes a range of property types, such as rental apartments, townhouses, condominiums, and detached houses. It is essential to the nation's economy since it promotes employment, construction activity, and the general accumulation of wealth. Numerous factors impact the market, such as immigration trends, population growth, interest rates, governmental regulations, and financial circumstances.

Major cities like Vancouver, Toronto, and Montreal have seen notable increases in their housing markets in recent years. Property values and demand have surged in these cities due to factors like low mortgage rates, rising populations, and foreign investment. However, there are worries about housing affordability as a result of this growth, especially for lower-class and first-time buyers.

On the other hand, some areas, especially those that depend more on resources or are more rural, may experience difficulties due to a drop in demand and falling property values. Variables, including industry shifts, population migration patterns, and economic downturns, may cause certain places to see slower growth or even a decline in home prices.

Numerous factors, such as land availability, the pace of development, and zoning laws, affect the housing supply in Canada. Due to zoning limitations and limited land availability, there may not be as many affordable housing options in high-demand locations. The mismatch between demand and supply has caused instability in the housing market and affordability issues in certain regions.

Impact of Recession on Mortgages

Recessions, defined by economic contractions and falling activity, can significantly impact the Canadian mortgage market. Most notably, the global financial crisis of 2008 profoundly affected the mortgage business and the housing market.

The Canadian real estate market saw a halt in activity and a decline in property values during the 2008 crisis. The collapse of the subprime mortgage market in the United States marked the beginning of the crisis, but its ramifications spread worldwide. The recession in Canada resulted in higher unemployment rates, stricter lending standards, and a drop in consumer confidence.

Mortgage foreclosures and delinquencies increased as several borrowers experienced difficulty making their mortgage payments during the recession. Financial institutions tightened lending standards, making it harder for applicants to be approved for mortgages. The inability of prospective buyers to obtain finance caused a brief halt in the residential property market.

Strong banking laws and cautious lending procedures in Canada helped lessen the effects of the 2008 crisis on the property market. Compared to other nations, the Canadian banking system—which is renowned for its stability and cautious approach—performed admirably. Government initiatives like the Insured Mortgage Purchase Program and the Canadian Secured Credit Facility stabilized the mortgage market and gave financial institutions liquidity.

3 TYPES OF MORTGAGES

Fixed-Rate Mortgages

One of Canada's most typical and well-liked mortgage product categories is fixed-rate mortgages. With a fixed-rate mortgage, monthly mortgage payments are stable and predictable because the interest rate stays the same for the duration of the loan.

Pros of Fixed-Rate Mortgages

1. *Consistency and Predictability:*

A fixed-rate mortgage has several benefits, chief among which are the consistency and predictability of monthly payments. Borrowers can better organize their finances and create budgets because they know how much they must pay each month.

Let's take an example of obtaining a 3% interest rate on a 25-year fixed mortgage. No matter how much the overall interest rate market fluctuates during the 25-year mortgage, your monthly payment will stay the same.

2. *Shelter against Interest Rate Increases:*

For the loan duration, borrowers with fixed-rate mortgages are protected against changes in interest rates. The rate and amount of the borrower's mortgage stay the same, even if market interest rates jump.

Assume, for example, that you had a fixed-rate mortgage with 4% interest while the market sees a 6% increase in interest rates. You won't have to deal with the financial strain of rising interest rates because your mortgage payment will remain constant.

3. *Financial Planning and Peace of Mind:*

Fixed-rate mortgages allow borrowers to precisely plan and budget their monthly spending, offering them financial planning and peace of mind. Those who like a regular payment schedule and wish to avoid any financial surprises will benefit from this consistency.

You can devote your cash to other bills or savings, knowing that your mortgage payment will not change, which gives you a sense of financial certainty.

Cons of Fixed-Rate Mortgages

1. Potentially Higher Initial Rates:
Fixed-rate mortgages frequently have higher interest rates than variable-rate mortgages. Borrowers might have to pay a higher interest rate for the security and consistency of fixed-rate loans.

Assume that the market rate for a fixed-rate mortgage is currently 4%, and the rate for a variable-rate mortgage is 3.5%. If you go for a fixed-rate mortgage, your interest rate will be slightly higher at first.

2. Restricted Flexibility:
Fixed-rate mortgages usually offer less flexibility than other mortgage options. The borrower's ability to take advantage of reduced interest rates or pay off the mortgage faster may be limited by limitations or penalties for early repayment or prepayment.

For example, you can pay a fee if you pay off your fixed-rate mortgage early on a mortgage with a prepayment penalty. This restricts your ability to pay off the mortgage early or make additional payments without incurring fees.

Adaptability to Varying Financial Circumstances

1. Risk-Averse Borrowers:
Fixed-rate mortgages are a good option for borrowers who value consistency over rate swings and are less at ease with them. A fixed-rate mortgage can be the best option if you value consistency and want to guarantee that your mortgage payments won't change over time.

A fixed-rate mortgage can offer the security and assurance needed for retirees with fixed incomes who wish to prevent unpleasant surprises regarding their mortgage payments.

2. Long-Term Homeowners:
A fixed-rate mortgage may be advantageous for borrowers who intend to remain in their residences for a considerable amount of time, such as those who buy their forever homes or have made local connections. A fixed-rate mortgage can be helpful if you can commit to

it for an extended period because of its stability and regular payments.

A fixed-rate mortgage can help with long-term financial planning if you intend to raise a family and live in your house for the next 30 years. It can give you the assurance that your mortgage payment will not fluctuate during that time.

Variable-Rate Mortgages

The interest rates on variable-rate mortgages, also called adjustable-rate mortgages (ARMs), can alter over the loan term in response to variations in a reference interest rate, usually the overnight lending rate set by the Bank of Canada. These mortgages frequently have a fixed-rate initial period, following which the interest rate is subject to periodic adjustments determined by the agreed-upon index and margin.

Pros of Variable-Rate Mortgages

1. Potential of Lower Starting Rates:
Compared to fixed-rate mortgages, variable-rate mortgages usually have lower starting interest rates. Lower monthly payments could result, perhaps saving money.

Assume that the market rate for a fixed-rate mortgage is currently 4%, and the rate for a variable-rate mortgage is 3%. You can initially obtain a cheaper interest rate by choosing a variable-rate mortgage, which will cut your monthly mortgage payments.

2. Options for Prepayment and Flexibility:
Compared to fixed-rate mortgages, variable-rate mortgages frequently offer borrowers greater flexibility. The options for prepayment may vary, such as lump sum payments or the ability to increase recurring installments without penalty. With this flexibility, borrowers can take advantage of future lower interest rates or accelerate their mortgage payoff.

You can pay off your variable-rate mortgage in full with your work bonus, lowering the amount owed and reducing the loan term.

Cons of Variable-Rate Mortgages

1. Exposure to Interest Rate Fluctuations:

The main risk associated with variable-rate mortgages is rising interest rates. If interest rates rise, borrowers may have to make larger mortgage payments, which would pressure their finances.

Assume you started with a 3% interest rate on a variable-rate mortgage. Your mortgage rate and monthly payments will adjust to reflect the new rate if the reference interest rate rises by 1%.

2. Uncertainty and challenges with budgeting:

Because borrowers are unable to forecast changes in interest rates in the future, variable-rate mortgages create uncertainty. This might make creating a budget more difficult, particularly for people who would rather receive consistent, dependable payments.

Variable-rate mortgages can be unsettling if you have a limited budget and would rather know how much your monthly mortgage payment will be. Because of this uncertainty, you may also find it challenging to arrange your finances.

Adaptability to Varying Financial Circumstances

1. Financially Flexible Borrowers:

Mortgages with variable rates might be a good fit for borrowers with the financial flexibility to modify their budget in response to future interest rate rises. They should be able to handle any prospective increases in mortgage payments and be at ease with the unpredictability of future changes in interest rates.

To benefit from potentially lower initial rates, a variable-rate mortgage can be a good choice if you have a steady income and enough resources to cover any increases in mortgage payments.

2. Shorter-Term Homeowners:

Variable-rate mortgages are an option for people who want to sell their properties or refinance in the near future. Even though interest rates may rise in the future, the initial reduced interest rates can still result in cost savings throughout the expected ownership duration.

If you intend to sell your house in the next five years, choosing a variable-rate mortgage with a five-year fixed-rate term will help you save on interest rates throughout the ownership period. This will help you stick to your immediate goals.

Hybrid Mortgages

Hybrid mortgages, also called combination mortgages, combine the characteristics of fixed-rate and variable-rate mortgages. These mortgages usually begin with a fixed interest rate for a predetermined amount of time, usually two to five years, after which they move to a variable rate for the duration of the loan.

Pros of Hybrid Mortgages

1. Initial Stability:

During the first few years of homeownership, borrowers can take advantage of a hybrid mortgage's fixed-rate period, which provides stability and predictability. This makes it easier for borrowers to budget their money and keep track of their monthly mortgage payments.

Let's say you obtain a hybrid mortgage with a five-year fixed-rate term. Your interest rate doesn't change during this time, giving your mortgage payments a sense of regularity and stability.

2. Possibility of Lower Rates:

Hybrid mortgages transfer to a variable rate at the end of the fixed-rate period, allowing reduced interest rates. This will enable borrowers to benefit from advantageous market circumstances and potential cost reductions.

Assume you have a hybrid mortgage with a variable rate based on the Bank of Canada's overnight lending rate after a five-year fixed-rate period. Your mortgage rate and monthly payments will drop if the overnight rate drops during the variable-rate term, potentially saving you money.

Who Qualifies for Hybrid Mortgage Benefits?

1. Homebuyers looking for flexibility and stability:

Hybrid mortgages are suitable for those who prefer stability in the early years of their mortgage but subsequently want to take advantage of possible cost savings from variable rates. With this type of mortgage, borrowers can benefit from fixed payment plans up front and then from changes in the market afterwards.

Young professionals buying their first home can benefit from a hybrid mortgage's regular payment schedule in the early years of their careers. The variable rate's potential savings can be helpful when they anticipate career advancement or pay increases.

2. *Those who are concerned about future trends in interest rates:*
Hybrid mortgages offer a middle ground for borrowers who want a balanced approach to their mortgage but are unsure about the direction of interest rates. They allow companies to benefit from fixed rates upfront while still having the flexibility to consider potential cost savings from variable rates down the road.

Suppose you would like to lock in a lower rate for the first few years but are unclear about the future course of interest rates. In that case, hybrid mortgages offer a flexible and well-balanced solution that can accommodate your uncertainties.

Open and Closed Mortgages

The terms and conditions of open and closed mortgages pertain to making additional payments or paying off the mortgage in full before the term ends. These conditions impact the borrower's penalty-free mortgage refinancing or prepayment options.

Distinctions Between Open and Closed Mortgages

1. Open Mortgages:
Open mortgages give borrowers more freedom since they don't charge extra for early repayment or additional payments. They are usually appropriate for borrowers who want to pay off their mortgage early or intend to make large lump-sum payments.

For instance, an open mortgage would enable you to make a sizable principal payment on your mortgage without facing penalties if you received a sizeable bequest or bonus at work.

2. Closed Mortgages:
Closed mortgages are subject to restrictions on early payment or

prepayment. Even though they frequently offer lower interest rates than open mortgages, borrowers who wish to make extra payments or pay off the mortgage before the term expires may be subject to fines or other limitations.

For instance, depending on the conditions of your loan agreement, you may be subject to fines or limits on early mortgage payments if you have a closed mortgage and choose to sell your home or refinance before the term ends.

Pros and Cons of Open Mortgages

Pros
- Flexibility to pay more without incurring fees.
- The choice to ultimately pay off the mortgage before the term expires

Cons
- Higher interest rates compared to closed mortgages.
- The flexibility feature could come with extra costs or charges.

Closed Mortgages

Pros
- Lower interest rates than open mortgages.
- Often offer more appealing rates and terms.

Cons
- There are limited options for increasing payments or early mortgage payoff.
- Prepayment may result in penalties or limitations.

Suitability to Varying Financial Circumstances

1. Open Mortgages
- *Self-employed people with irregular income:*

Open mortgages offer the option to make lump sum payments during periods of higher income, making them appropriate for people with fluctuating incomes.

- *Borrowers who plan to sell their homes soon:*

If you intend to sell your house soon, selecting an open mortgage gives you the flexibility to make extra payments and lower the remaining sum prior to the sale.

2. Closed Mortgages
- *Borrowers shopping for lower interest rates:*

Closed mortgages are a desirable choice for people trying to reduce their mortgage expenses because they often have lower interest rates.

- *Borrowers who prefer consistency and a predetermined payment plan:*

Because they offer a fixed monthly payment schedule, closed mortgages are a good option for borrowers who want consistent monthly payments and don't plan to make large prepayments.

Other Specialized Mortgage Types

Other customized mortgage options address other borrower requirements besides fixed-rate, variable-rate, hybrid, open-end, and closed mortgages.

1. High-Ratio Mortgages:

High-ratio mortgages are offered for borrowers who can afford to put less than 20% down on the purchase price of their property. Mortgage insurance is necessary for these loans to shield the lender from default risks. They allow borrowers to enter the home market with minimal down payments.

For example, you can apply for a high-ratio mortgage if you have a 10% down payment on a house, but you will have to pay for mortgage insurance, which covers the lender in the event of a failure.

2. Reverse Mortgages:

For homeowners, 55 years or older, reverse mortgages provide access to a portion of their home's value without requiring them to make monthly mortgage payments. The loan's interest is paid back when the homeowner either sells the house or passes away, and it accumulates over time.

Let's say you are an elderly homeowner with a sizable equity stake in your home. Then, instead of making monthly mortgage payments, you can use a reverse mortgage to obtain assets for retirement or other financial needs.

4 CHOOSING THE RIGHT MORTGAGE

Factors to Consider When Choosing a Mortgage Product

Selecting the appropriate mortgage is an important choice that must be carefully considered. To ensure the mortgage fits with your long-term plans, risk tolerance, and financial goals, it's critical to evaluate a number of criteria. Consider the following important factors:

1. *Interest Rates*

Examine the interest rates that various lenders are offering. The total cost of the mortgage can be significantly impacted by even a slight variation in interest rates. Depending on whether you choose stability or potential cost savings, evaluate whether you want a fixed-rate, variable-rate, or hybrid mortgage.

2. *Mortgage Term*

The mortgage term refers to the life of the mortgage arrangement. Standard terms are one, three, five, or ten years; however, more prolonged terms could be offered. While longer terms give stability but may have higher rates, shorter terms usually offer lower rates but have more regular renewals.

3. *Down Payment*

Figure out the amount of the down payment that you can afford to make. Typically, a down payment of 5% of the home's purchase price is required, but a larger down payment can lower your mortgage amount, save interest expenses, and remove the need for mortgage insurance.

4. *Amortization Period*

The amortization period refers to the time needed to pay off the mortgage in full, usually lasting between 15 and 30 years—a longer amortization term results in lower monthly payments but greater total interest expenses. When choosing an amortization time, consider your financial situation and future goals.

5. *Monthly Payments*

Make a budget and compare the monthly payments of several mortgage options. Ensure the payments fit your income, spending, and other financial commitments. They should also be reasonable.

6. Prepayment Options

Think about whether you want the freedom to pay more or if you want to be able to increase your regular payments without incurring penalties. Prepayment rights are a feature of some mortgages that can help you pay off your debt more quickly and reduce your interest expenses.

Assessing Individual Financial Goals and Risk Tolerance

Choosing the ideal mortgage requires understanding your risk tolerance and specific financial goals. Think about the following:

1. Homeownership Plans:
Establish the duration of your intended stay at the property. A shorter-term mortgage or flexible prepayment options might be more appropriate if you plan to move within a few years. A stable mortgage with a longer duration can be more suitable if you intend to stay.

2. Financial Flexibility:
Consider how flexible your finances are to accommodate any future adjustments to interest rates, higher payment amounts, or unforeseen costs. Consider your emergency funds, work prospects, and income consistency. This will assist in deciding whether you would be better off with a fixed-rate mortgage or a variable-rate mortgage.

3. Risk Tolerance:
Consider the degree of risk you can tolerate when it comes to changes in interest rates. A fixed-rate mortgage can be better if you want stability and don't want to worry about future payment hikes. A variable-rate mortgage might be a better option if you wish to have cost savings during low interest rates and can handle some volatility.

Understanding Mortgage Terms and Conditions

Make sure you read and comprehend the terms and conditions of the mortgage agreement before committing to one. Among the crucial elements to consider are:

1. **Prepayment Penalties**

Verify whether there are any penalties associated with making early mortgage payments or paying the loan off before the term expires. Different lenders have different repayment penalties, so it's important to know what they would cost if you want to make larger payments or pay off your mortgage sooner.

2. **Portability and Assumability**

Find out if the mortgage is assumable or portable. Assumability enables a buyer to take over the current mortgage when buying your property. At the same time, it allows you to transfer the mortgage to a new property if you wish to move. These characteristics may be helpful if you intend to sell in the future or if you foresee changing your housing needs.

3. **Refinancing Options**

Determine whether the lender offers refinancing options. Refinancing allows you to renegotiate the terms of your mortgage, possibly gaining access to better rates or conditions. Knowing your refinancing alternatives can be helpful if you want to tap the equity in your home or expect changes in interest rates.

Affordability and The Mortgage Pre-Approval Process

An essential first step in the home-buying process is figuring out your finances and getting a mortgage pre-approval. Consider the following:

1. Affordability Assessment:

Add up all of the expenses associated with your home, including your mortgage, insurance, property taxes, and any potential condo fees. Compare these costs to your monthly income to be sure they are within a fair range. Essentially, lenders evaluate borrower affordability using the debt-to-income ratio.

2. Mortgage Pre-Approval:

Obtain a lender's pre-approval for a mortgage before you start looking at properties. A pre-approval strengthens your position when making offers on houses, assists you in figuring out how much mortgage you can afford, and helps you create a reasonable spending plan.

3. Documentation Requirements:

Gather the required paperwork for the pre-approval procedure, such as proof of income, employment verification, bank statements, and information about your assets and liabilities. If these materials are prepared, the procedure will go more quickly.

How To Compare Mortgage Products And Lenders

Take into account the following tips while comparing mortgage options and lenders:

1. Shop around:

Get mortgage quotations from many lenders to compare interest rates, conditions, and fees. Shopping around lets you get the most attractive deal that meets your needs.

2. Read the fine print:

Analyze all of the information and documentation that the lender has provided. Be mindful of any unstated costs, fines, or conditions that could impact your mortgage transaction.

3. Consider additional services:

Assess the lender's array of services, including customer service, online account management, and accessibility. A lender who provides convenient tools and outstanding customer service might improve your mortgage experience.

4. Seek professional advice:

Speak with a financial advisor or mortgage broker for assistance navigating the mortgage market. They can offer professional advice. They can help you weigh your alternatives and choose which mortgage plan best suits your requirements.

5 MORTGAGE PROTECTION AND RISK MITIGATION

The Significance of Mortgage Insurance

Mortgage insurance safeguards lenders and borrowers in the case of default. It offers both parties to a mortgage transaction risk minimization and financial stability. When applying for a mortgage, it is essential to understand mortgage insurance and its significance.

1. Mortgage Default Insurance:

Homebuyers who make a down payment of less than 20% of the purchase price must obtain mortgage default insurance, sometimes called high-ratio mortgage insurance. This insurance shields the lender against possible damages if the borrower fails to pay the mortgage.

2. Canada Mortgage and Housing Corporation (CMHC):

Mortgage loan insurance is provided by the federal agency Canada Mortgage and Housing Corporation. CMHC is the largest provider of mortgage default insurance in Canada. However, commercial insurers like Canada Guaranty and Genworth Financial Canada also provide equivalent products.

Benefits of Mortgage Insurance

a. *Enables Homeownership:*

Mortgage insurance makes homeownership more accessible by enabling borrowers to buy a property with a lower down payment, especially for first-time buyers or people with limited savings.

b. *Protects Lenders:*

Mortgage insurance protects lenders from default risk, facilitating their ability to lend to borrowers with smaller down payments.

c. *Competitive Interest Rates:*

Lenders are more likely to offer competitive interest rates due to the additional protection that mortgage insurance provides.

Role of CMHC (Canada Mortgage and Housing Corporation)

CMHC significantly impacts the mortgage market and the housing sector in Canada. Among its primary responsibilities are:

1. Mortgage Loan Insurance:
CMHC provides mortgage loan insurance to borrowers with less than a 20% down payment. This insurance gives borrowers access to mortgage financing at affordable interest rates and shields lenders from the danger of default.

2. Research and Information:
CMHC studies and analyzes affordability, demography, and housing market developments. It offers the public, legislators, and business experts valuable information and insights.

3. Housing Policy and Program Development:
CMHC is essential in formulating housing policies and programs to promote affordable housing initiatives, homelessness prevention, and sustainable housing development across Canada.

4. Housing Research Grants:
To promote cooperation and the growth of knowledge, CMHC provides funds to encourage research and innovation in housing-related sectors.

Strategies For Reducing Mortgage Risks

Although mortgage insurance offers security, there are other measures that borrowers can take to lower their mortgage risk. The following are some tactics:

1. Larger Down Payment:
Raising your down payment lowers the total amount financed and the dangers involved. A higher down payment may lead to a lower loan-to-value (LTV) ratio, which could cut your interest rate and eliminate the requirement for mortgage insurance.

2. Building an Emergency Fund:
Setting up an emergency fund can reduce the financial risks connected with unforeseen spending, job loss, or changes in circumstances. In hard

times, having a buffer can provide peace of mind and enable you to keep up with your mortgage payments.

3. Debt-to-income ratio:

You may maintain a good debt-to-income ratio by making your total debt obligations—including the mortgage payment—manageable. A lower debt-to-income ratio lowers the default risk and indicates improved financial stability.

4. Regular Mortgage Payments:

Making your mortgage payments on time every month contributes to equity development and keeping a good credit history. This lowers the chance of default and indicates fiscal discipline.

Exploring the Benefits of Fixed-Rate Mortgages

Fixed-rate mortgages provide certain advantages that help with risk minimization and mortgage protection:

- *Stability and Predictability:* With a fixed-rate mortgage, your interest rate is locked for the duration of the mortgage, giving your monthly payments stability and predictability. This makes financial planning and budgeting more accurate.

- *Protection against Interest Rate Increases:* Mortgages with fixed rates protect borrowers from increases in interest rates. Your mortgage rate doesn't fluctuate even if market rates do, giving you peace of mind and averting any unexpected payment outcomes.

- *Long-Term Planning:* Fixed-rate mortgages are a good option for borrowers who would rather have a long-term savings plan. Regular payments make better long-term planning possible, freeing up money for other financial obligations and aspirations.

Lessons from the 2008 Global Financial Crisis

The 2008 financial crisis significantly impacted the housing market, and in certain areas, it collapsed. This experience can help lenders and borrowers make wise decisions in the future when the economy is low. Important lessons learned include:

a. **Responsible Lending and Borrowing:**
Appropriate lending and borrowing practices, such as careful affordability assessments and reasonable down payments, decrease mortgage default risk.

b. **Diversification of Investments:**
Avoid using real estate as your only investment plan. During economic downturns, diversifying your financial portfolio can help distribute risk and provide a cushion.

d. **Monitoring Market Conditions:**
Keep up with economic statistics, housing market developments, and interest rate swings to make informed mortgage finance and homeownership decisions.

6 UNDERSTANDING RECESSIONS AND MORTGAGES

Overview of the 2008 Global Financial Crisis

The global financial crisis of 2008 marked a turning point in the development of modern finance. Borrowers must comprehend the origins, effects, and lessons learned from this crisis to make wise judgments about their mortgages.

Causes of the Crisis

The 2008 financial crisis had multiple underlying causes that contributed to its magnitude and global impact. These causes included:

a. **Housing Bubble:**
In the United States, a historic housing bubble characterized by inflated property values, speculative purchases, and risky financing methods occurred. The substantial increase in subprime mortgages granted to borrowers with bad credit histories contributed significantly.

b. **Securitization and Complex Financial Instruments:**
Financial institutions packaged and sold mortgage-backed securities (MBS) to investors, often based on subprime mortgages. Because of their complexity, it was challenging to ascertain the actual risk exposure of these financial products.

c. **Leverage and Excessive Risk-Taking:**
Financial institutions and investors had to take out large loans because they financed their investments with excessive leverage. As a result, they became more vulnerable to declines in the real estate market.

e. **Regulatory Failures:**
Regulatory oversight and enforcement did not sufficiently address the hazards connected to the housing market and intricate financial instruments. Little regulation of financial institutions resulted in systemic risks.

Impact on the Canadian Housing Market

While the US property market did not collapse as severely as the

Canadian housing market, it nonetheless encountered many difficulties during the crisis. The principal effects comprised:

a. ***Property value drop:*** In Canada, there was a pause and, in certain areas, a drop in housing prices. Even though the fall was not as bad as it was in the United States, it nonetheless affected homeowners' equity.

b. ***Decreased Housing Sales:*** The financial crisis reduced housing sales activity as credit became more difficult to obtain and buyer confidence dropped. The real estate market slowed down as buyers grew increasingly wary.

c. ***Foreclosures and Mortgage Defaults:*** The crisis led to a rise in these events, but at a slower pace in Canada than in the United States. This was partially due to Canada's more stringent lending guidelines and cautious mortgage procedures.

Impacts on the Canadian Housing Market and Mortgages

The Canadian housing and mortgage markets were affected by the 2008 financial crisis in several ways, both directly and indirectly:

1. Mortgage Availability and Stringency

Following the crisis, lenders tightened their standards and increased their prudence when approving mortgages. They established more income verification standards, higher credit score requirements, and greater down payments to reduce risk.

2. **Interest Rates**

Global central banks, including the Bank of Canada, responded to the crisis by enacting monetary policies to boost the economy. Among other things, borrowing rates were sharply lowered to record lows. Reduced interest rates helped the property market, promoted economic recovery, and made borrowing more accessible.

3. **Housing Affordability**

In many Canadian regions, the financial crisis resulted in a brief decline in housing prices, making homes more accessible to potential buyers. This allowed buyers to enter the market or upgrade at more affordable prices.

4. **Market Stability**

Throughout the crisis, the Canadian property market displayed resilience. Even with its setbacks, it rebounded more swiftly than other nations. Elements including stringent laws, a robust financial system, and cautious lending practices facilitated the market's stability.

Lessons Learned and Implications for Future Mortgage Decisions

Essential lessons from the 2008 financial crisis might help borrowers make wise mortgage decisions in challenging economic times:

1. **Responsible Borrowing and Lending**

The crisis made proper lending and borrowing practices even more crucial. Borrowers must evaluate their financial situation thoroughly, ensure they can afford their mortgage payments, and refrain from taking on more debt than they can manage.

2. **Diversification of Investments**

Over-reliance on real estate as the only source of income during recessions might put borrowers at greater risk. Investment portfolio diversification, which includes a variety of assets and financial instruments, can reduce risk and promote stability.

3. **Mortgage Stress Testing**

Mortgage stress tests can assist borrowers in determining their resilience to monetary setbacks. These tests assess their capacity to make mortgage payments at higher interest rates to ensure they can manage future rate hikes and preserve their financial stability.

4. **Long-Term Financial Planning**

The crisis made long-term financial planning even more crucial. When choosing a mortgage, borrowers should consider their risk tolerance, stability, and financial objectives. A clear financial strategy can help reduce risks and navigate turbulent economic times.

The Role of Government Interventions and Regulations

Governments frequently step in to stabilize the housing market and lessen the effects on borrowers during economic downturns. Among the crucial actions and interventions are:

1. **Regulatory Changes**

Governments may impose new restrictions or strengthen existing ones to encourage prudent lending and borrowing practices. These modifications are intended to lower systemic risks, improve consumer safety, and guarantee the financial system's stability. Stress testing, more stringent mortgage qualification guidelines, and enhanced financial institution supervision are a few examples.

2. **Monetary Policy Adjustments**

Central banks can use monetary policy tools to influence interest rates and provide economic stimulus during recessions. Lowering interest rates makes borrowing more affordable, stimulates economic activity, and supports the housing market.

Case Study of the 1991 Downturn: The Canadian Experience with Recessions and Mortgages

Another case study on the effects of economic downturns on mortgages is the Canadian recession of 1991. Gaining an understanding of the developments and results throughout this time might provide borrowers with essential insights:

Background of the 1991 Recession

A worse global economy, rising interest rates, and a significant rise in state debt were the leading causes of Canada's recession in 1991. The nation experienced a sharp economic decline, elevated jobless rates, and a collapse in the real estate sector.

Impact on the Mortgage Industry

The 1991 recession significantly impacted the Canadian mortgage market. Mortgage defaults rose along with the sharp increase in mortgage rates, which put borrowers in financial difficulty. Both sales and property values fell in the housing market.

Government Responses and Effects on the Mortgage Market

The Canadian government responded to the 1991 recession by enacting policies to boost the economy and stabilize the housing market. To encourage economic recovery, interest rates were progressively lowered through fiscal programs. These initiatives supported mortgage affordability and bolstered confidence.

Key Takeaways for Mortgage Borrowers During Economic Downturns

1. The Importance of Budgetary Planning

The 1991 recession underscored the importance of carefully planning one's finances. This entails drafting an extensive budget that considers debt management, savings, income, and expenses. A clear understanding of one's financial status might act as a safety net against unanticipated events during economic downturns.

2. Mortgage Affordability:

It is critical to keep mortgages affordable, particularly in times of economic uncertainty. The maximum mortgage amount should be a prudent percentage of the borrower's income. These guarantee homeowners are not overly burdened and may continue making payments without experiencing undue hardship during difficult economic times.

3. Interest Rate Fluctuations:

Borrowers should be aware of the possibility of rate increases and consider fixed-rate mortgages to guarantee manageable payments. On the other hand, borrowers can prepare for potential rate changes by comprehending the terms of adjustable-rate mortgages (ARMs).

4. Housing Market Dynamics:

During recessions, the housing market can undergo notable changes that impact equity and property values. In light of these possible developments, homeowners should consider their capacity to sell or buy real estate, home equity lines of credit, and refinancing options.

5. Emergency Preparedness:

One essential element of financial resilience is an emergency reserve. To protect themselves from losing their jobs or experiencing other economic setbacks, mortgage debtors should try to save several months' worth of living expenses, which includes their mortgage payments.

6. Government Programs and Assistance:

Knowing about government help programs can be a lifesaver in challenging economic situations. Programs created to assist homeowners needing financial assistance can stop foreclosure and offer momentary respite.

7. Long-Term Perspective:

Lastly, it's critical to keep a long-term view. Economic downturns are usually cyclical, with recovery occurring afterward. By remaining informed and organized, mortgage borrowers can handle these times more skillfully and emerge in a stable financial position.

By learning from previous recessions, like the one that occurred in 1991, mortgage borrowers can better prepare themselves to meet fiscal challenges and make decisions that preserve financial stability and property retention.

7 NAVIGATING THE MORTGAGE PROCESS

Step-by-Step Guide to Obtaining a Mortgage

Getting a mortgage involves several procedures, all of which must be carefully planned and thought through. This section offers a comprehensive, step-by-step guide to assist potential homebuyers in successfully navigating the mortgage application and approval process.

1. **Establish your budget**

   Assessing your financial status and determining how much you can afford to borrow should come first. Consider your earnings, outgoings, and any current debts or financial obligations. Use online mortgage calculators or consult a mortgage expert to determine your affordability.

2. **Shop mortgage options**

   Examine the various mortgage options available to you. Consider terms, interest rates, repayment options, and future interest rate changes. Being aware of the different mortgage possibilities will ease your decision-making process.

3. **Get pre-approved**

   Get a lender's mortgage pre-approval before beginning your house hunt. A lender will assess your financial history and tell you an estimated loan amount you qualify for during pre-approval. It gives you a better grasp of your budget and fortifies your position as a buyer.

4. **Gather the required documents.**

   Put together the supporting documentation for your loan application. Standard documents include identification, tax reports, bank statements, employment verification, proof of income, and details of any assets or obligations.

5. **Submit the mortgage application**

   Complete the mortgage application you received from your lender. Make sure all the information is up to date-and accurate. After that, submit the application and the necessary documentation.

6. **Mortgage underwriting and review**

   Once the lender receives your application, they will review and assess the information you submit. The property you intend to purchase will be evaluated, and your employment, income, and credit history will be verified. This process may take time because the lender will thoroughly review your application.

7. Appraisal and property evaluation

The lender may arrange for an appraisal to determine the fair market value of the property you intend to purchase. The appraiser will assess the property's size, location, condition, and comparable sales in the neighbourhood. The assessment helps the lender ensure that the loan amount and the property's value are in line.

8. Mortgage approval and offer

If the lender approves your application and the property appraisal is favourable, you will be approved for a mortgage. Next, the lender will present you with an offer, including the terms, interest rate, repayment schedule, and additional costs or requirements.

9. Legal process and documentation

Employ a real estate lawyer or notary public to handle the legal requirements of the mortgage transaction. They will review the mortgage agreement, make sure all legal requirements are met, and help with closing.

10. Closing the mortgage

Before the closing, review the mortgage papers again. Plan to cover all closing costs, including applicable taxes, legal fees, and other charges related to land transfer. Sign the necessary documents and complete the money transfer to finalize the mortgage.

Documentation and Requirements

The mortgage application process requires specific proof to validate your eligibility and financial data. The standard documentation and requirements that lenders usually need are listed in the following section:

1. ***Identification:*** Present valid identification, such as a driver's license, passport, or other official identification.

2. ***Proof of Income:*** To assess your capacity to pay back your mortgage, lenders require evidence of your income. These could be current pay stubs, tax returns, and employment letters. Self-

employed people could also be required to submit additional documentation, including business financial statements.

3. **Employment Verification:** Lenders may contact your company to verify your employment details, including your consistent earnings and job security.

4. **Bank Statements:** Provide bank statements with a few months' worth of transactions so lenders can evaluate your spending patterns, savings, and outstanding commitments.

5. **Assets and Liability Details:** It is necessary to disclose all assets, including stocks and real estate, and any ongoing debts, such as loans and credit card debt. Lenders assess your overall financial status using this information.

6. **Property Information:** Lenders may also require your preferred property's address, purchase price, and expected closing date, among other details.

Mortgage Application Tips

To increase your chances of getting your mortgage application approved, consider the following tips:

1. Improve your credit score:

A better credit score makes it more likely that you will be accepted for a better mortgage with a lower interest rate. To improve your credit score, pay off your existing debt, make your payments on schedule, and avoid obtaining new credit.

2. Minimize new credit activity:

Don't take out new credit or make big purchases before applying for a mortgage. Lenders prefer it when borrowers exhibit consistent and predictable financial behaviour.

3. Keep financial records organized:

Organize your tax returns, bank statements, and pay stubs. This will expedite the application process and enable prompt recovery of the necessary documents.

4. Avoid large deposits or withdrawals:
Significant deposits or withdrawals from your bank accounts that happen out of the blue could raise questions during underwriting. Continue with your regular banking schedule, and be prepared to explain any significant transactions.

5. Be truthful and accurate:
Provide accurate and correct information throughout the application procedure. False information or the omission of crucial elements might result in serious repercussions, including accusations of mortgage fraud.

Common Pitfalls to Avoid During the Mortgage Process

The mortgage application process can be challenging to navigate and to prevent any issues, borrowers should be aware of the following common pitfalls:

1. Overextending Your Budget
Refrain from taking on more debt than you can manage. Consider all of the expenditures associated with homeownership, including upkeep, insurance, and property taxes, in addition to the mortgage payment.

2. Neglecting the Pre-Approval Process
Obtaining pre-approval for a mortgage fortifies your position as a buyer and helps you better understand your budget. You could be disappointed if you skip this step and later find out you're not eligible for the desired loan amount.

3. Ignoring Other Lenders and Mortgage Options
You shouldn't entirely go for the first mortgage offer you receive. Instead, shop around and compare mortgage offers from several lenders to ensure you get the best terms and rates possible.

4. Inadequate Research on Closing Costs
Appraisal fees, property transfer taxes, and legal fees are just a few closing costs that could rise quickly. Remember to factor these costs into your budget.

5. Making Major Financial Changes During the Process
Avoid making significant life changes throughout the mortgage process, such as taking on more debt, switching jobs, or making large

purchases. These modifications could jeopardize or delay your approval, affecting your eligibility.

Closing the Mortgage and Post-Mortgage Considerations

The homeownership process starts once the last mortgage procedure is completed and the mortgage is finalized. Critical considerations that should be made both during and following the closure process are outlined in this section:

1. *Finalize Closing Costs:*

You should ensure sufficient funds to cover all closing charges, including attorney fees, taxes on land transactions, and any other pertinent costs.

2. *Review Mortgage Documents:*

Examine the mortgage documentation thoroughly before signing. Look for the terms, interest rate, repayment schedule, and any additional fees.

3. *Mortgage Payment Setup:*

Decide on a mortgage payment plan that is within your financial means. Consider automatic or pre-authorized debits to ensure consistent and timely payments.

4. *Ongoing Financial Management:*

Once you have a mortgage, maintain your good financial habits. Keep your mortgage payments on track, save additional money, and budget for any expenses related to becoming a homeowner.

5. *Regular Mortgage Reviews:*

In light of your changing goals and financial status, regularly review your mortgage to determine whether it still makes sense. See a mortgage expert to learn about your options for lowering your interest rate, refinancing, or making other changes.

8 BUILDING WEALTH THROUGH MORTGAGES

Mortgages are valuable tools for building wealth in Canada but must be used carefully. In this chapter, we'll discuss using mortgages for future planning, real estate investing, and debt reduction.

Overview of How Mortgages Can Be Used to Build Wealth in Canada

There are two main ways you can use mortgages to boost wealth in Canada:

1. **Investing in real estate:**

Purchasing a home with a mortgage amounts to borrowing money for an asset you hope will appreciate in value over time. It is possible to grow wealth in Canada by carefully choosing homes that are expected to appreciate in value.

2. **Debt reduction:**

One way to consolidate high-interest debt into a single, lower-interest loan is to utilize a mortgage to pay down a credit card or student loan debt. Over time, the savings on interest payments can provide you with more funds for savings or investments.

Strategies for Leveraging Mortgages to Invest in Real Estate in Canada

Mortgage financing for real estate ventures can be done in several ways. Some commonly used strategies are:

(i) **Buy-and-hold**

Buying a property and staying in it for a long time is the most straightforward strategy. As the value of the property increases, you will accumulate equity—the difference between the home's value and the amount you still owe on the mortgage.

Consider the following situation: you purchase a home for $500,000 ($100,000) and contribute 20% of the price. Your mortgage would run you $400,000. If the home appreciated to $700,000, your equity would be $200,000.

You can then choose to either use the equity to buy another home or sell it and pocket the profit.

(ii)   House hacking
By renting out a part of your home to tenants, you can use this technique to pay down your mortgage. This could be a great strategy to increase your wealth if you find tenants willing to pay a fair rent.

For example, let's assume you put down a 20% down payment of $100,000 to purchase a $500,000 property. That would be $400,000 for your mortgage. Your mortgage payments would be paid if you rented half the property for $2,000 monthly.

This type of approach can help first-time home buyers by allowing them to acquire a more expensive home than they usually could.

(iii)   Flipping
The goal is to buy a house, make renovations, and then resell it for a profit. This process has a high risk and labour component, but it has the potential to be very rewarding.

Consider this scenario: You purchase a property for $500,000 but need $100,000 in improvements. After the upgrades, the property is worth $700,000. If you sold the house for $700,000, you would have made $100,000.

But before you start flipping houses, you need to do your homework because there's a higher chance of losing money.

(iv)   Wholesaling
This involves identifying properties at a discount to market value and profitably reselling them to other investors. This method requires less labour than flipping and has less risk.

For example, you find a property valued at $500,000, but the seller is only ready to sell it for $400,000. After that, you might make a $100,000 profit by selling the property to another investor for $500,000.

This strategy is a good option for beginner real estate investors because it requires less knowledge and experience.

9 THE FUTURE OF MORTGAGES IN CANADA

The mortgage market in Canada is dynamic, with new advancements and trends developing regularly. Some noteworthy advancements and patterns that could impact the future of mortgages in Canada are outlined below:

1. **The emergence of digital mortgages**

Digital mortgages are becoming increasingly popular because they provide borrowers a more straightforward and efficient experience. They offer lower interest rates than traditional mortgages and include an online application and approval process.

According to research by the Canadian Mortgage and Housing Corporation, for example, the average interest rate on a digital mortgage was 0.25% lower than that of a conventional mortgage.

2. **The growth of alternative lending**

Alternative lending is growing in popularity in the mortgage industry because it gives borrowers access to funds they might not be able to obtain from traditional lenders. Alternative lenders offer a wide range of products, including bad credit mortgages, mortgages for self-employed borrowers, and mortgages for borrowers with non-traditional income.

For example, a survey by the Financial Consumer Agency of Canada found that the number of alternative mortgage loans increased by 40% between 2016 and 2017.

3. **The increasing use of data analytics**

Data analytics plays a more significant role in the mortgage market, as lenders use it to make better decisions about who and how much to lend. By utilizing data analytics, lenders can identify high-risk borrowers and better target their marketing efforts.

An example of this is that lenders who implement data analytics are more likely to grant loans to borrowers with solid credit histories, according to a survey conducted by the Canadian Bankers Association.

Predictions for the Future of Mortgages

Although there is uncertainty regarding the future of mortgages in Canada, several indicators suggest that the business will likely change over the next few years. The following are some significant forecasts regarding the future of mortgages:

1. **Mortgages will become more digital:**
The growing popularity of digital mortgages can be attributed to their ability to provide borrowers with a more straightforward and streamlined experience. For example, projections indicate that half of all mortgages will be digital by 2025.

2. **Alternative lending will continue to grow:**
Alternative lending is expected to grow. By 2025, it is predicted to be responsible for 10% of all mortgages, as it gives borrowers access to money they might not be able to acquire from traditional lenders.

3. **Data analytics will become even more critical:**
The mortgage industry will see a further increase in the use of data analytics as lenders utilize data to make more informed judgments about who and how much to lend. By 2025, 75% of lenders are predicted to use data analytics in their lending choices.

4. **Mortgage rates will fluctuate:**
Mortgage rates are impacted by several variables, such as the demand for mortgages, the status of the Canadian economy, and the level of interest rates in the US. They are expected to change over the next several years. Long-term mortgage rates, however, are anticipated to stay relatively low.

Regulatory Changes and Their Potential Impact on Borrowers

Regulations about the mortgage business are also prone to change, which may significantly affect borrowers. The following are a few significant regulatory adjustments that have been made recently:

- **The introduction of stress tests:**
Stress testing was made mandatory for all mortgage borrowers in Canada in 2017. To prevent loan default if interest rates increase, these stress tests require that borrowers be eligible for a mortgage at a higher

interest rate. Although the stress test's current rate is set at 5.25%, an increase could occur in the future.

- **The tightening of lending standards:**
Lenders have tightened their lending requirements in recent years, making it harder for borrowers to qualify for a mortgage. This is caused by several factors, such as the growing housing expense and the elevated default risk. In the future, it's feasible that loan requirements will be even more stringent.

How to Stay Informed and Adapt to Evolving Mortgage Landscapes Because the mortgage market changes, borrowers must keep up with the newest developments. There are several ways of remaining knowledgeable, such as:

- **Reading industry publications:** A number of industry journals, including Canadian Mortgage Trends and Mortgage Professional Canada, provide regular updates on the mortgage sector.

- **Attending industry events:** Borrowers can learn about the newest developments and trends at several industry events.

- **Talking to a mortgage professional:** A mortgage professional can provide borrowers with individualized advice and help on the mortgage market.

By keeping up to date with the latest trends and developments in the mortgage business, borrowers may make educated decisions regarding their mortgage and safeguard themselves against potential risks.

CONCLUSION

Although the future of mortgages in Canada is uncertain, several indicators show that the business will likely change over the next few years. By being aware of the significant advancements and trends in the mortgage business, borrowers may be ready for the future and make wise decisions about their mortgages.

Here are some additional tips for staying informed about the future of mortgages:

a. **Track industry news and trends:** Several websites and magazines, including Canadian Mortgage Trends and Mortgage Professional Canada, provide information about the mortgage sector. To be informed of the newest developments, you can also follow prominent personalities in the industry on social media.

b. **Speak with your mortgage specialist:** A great place to learn about the mortgage market is from your mortgage specialist. They can provide personalized guidance and direction based on your unique circumstances.

c. **Be ready to adjust:** The mortgage industry is constantly changing, so adjusting to new circumstances is critical. This entails being open to novel concepts and items and being prepared to adjust your mortgage plan when circumstances demand.

APPENDIX
Glossary of Mortgage-Related Terms

Amortization: the procedure of gradually repaying a loan.

APR: Annual Percentage Rate. The annual percentage rate, or APR, represents the overall cost of a loan.

Closing costs: the costs incurred when a mortgage loan is closed.

Down payment: the amount of money spent in cash toward acquiring a property.

Fixed-rate mortgage: a mortgage loan with an interest rate fixed for the duration of the loan.

Interest rate: the total interest that a loan is subject to.

Mortgage: a loan that has real estate as security.

Prepayment penalty: an expense incurred by borrowers who pay off their mortgage loans early.

Term: the duration of a mortgage loan.

Variable-rate mortgage: an adjustable interest rate mortgage loan.

Foreclosure: This is the process by which a bank or mortgage lender seizes property that is in default, frequently against the homeowner's will.

Additional Resources and References

Canadian Mortgage and Housing Corporation (CMHC): CMHC is a federal Crown corporation that offers lenders mortgage insurance.

Financial Consumer Agency of Canada (FCAC): The FCAC is an independent government body that protects customers' rights in the banking industry.

Mortgage Professionals Canada: Mortgage Professionals Canada is a national association of mortgage professionals.

Canadian Mortgage Trends: Canadian Mortgage Trends is a monthly publication that covers the mortgage industry.
Helpful Websites, Tools, and Calculators
CMHC's Mortgage Calculator: This calculator can help you estimate your monthly mortgage payments.

FCAC's Mortgage Calculator: This is a calculator that helps you compare different mortgage options.

Mortgage Professionals Canada's Mortgage Calculator: This is a calculator that helps you find a mortgage professional in your region.

Government of Canada: There is a section on mortgages on the Government of Canada's website that offers details on things like mortgage rates, mortgage insurance, and types.

Ratehub: Ratehub is a website that allows you to compare mortgage rates from different lenders.

NOTES

THE MORTGAGE MASTERY SYSTEM

THE MORTGAGE MASTERY SYSTEM

THE MORTGAGE MASTERY SYSTEM

THE MORTGAGE MASTERY SYSTEM

www.ingramcontent.com/pod-product-compliance
Lightning Source LLC
Chambersburg PA
CBHW072137070526
44585CB00016B/1724